Up

by Bridget Carpenter

A SAMUEL FRENCH ACTING EDITION

SAMUEL FRENCH

FOUNDED 1830

NEW YORK HOLLYWOOD LONDON TORONTO

SAMUELFRENCH.COM

ISBN 978-0-573-66374-1   Printed in U.S.A.   #23619

MUSIC USE NOTE

Licensees are solely responsible for obtaining formal written permission from copyright owners to use copyrighted music in the performance of this play and are strongly cautioned to do so. If no such permission is obtained by the licensee, then the licensee must use only original music that the licensee owns and controls. Licensees are solely responsible and liable for all music clearances and shall indemnify the copyright owners of the play and their licensing agent, Samuel French, Inc., against any costs, expenses, losses and liabilities arising from the use of music by licensees.

IMPORTANT BILLING AND CREDIT REQUIREMENTS

All producers of *UP* *must* give credit to the Author of the Play in all programs distributed in connection with performances of the Play, and in all instances in which the title of the Play appears for the purposes of advertising, publicizing or otherwise exploiting the Play and/or a production. The name of the Author *must* appear on a separate line on which no other name appears, immediately following the title and *must* appear in size of type not less than fifty percent of the size of the title type.

In addition the following credit *must* be given in all programs and publicity information distributed in association with this piece:

Up was commissioned, developed and received its World Premiere in May 2003 at Perseverance Theatre, Douglas, Alaska (Peter Dubois, Artistic Director)

CHARACTERS

WALTER GRIFFIN, 44
HELEN GRIFFIN, 38
MIKEY GRIFFIN, 15
MARIA, 16
AUNT CHRIS, 35-55
PHILIPPE PETIT, 35-50
STUDENT, 16
FIREFIGHTER, 20-30
HELEN'S MOTHER, 50
STUDENT, UPS MAN, and FIREFIGHTER are played by the actor who plays Philippe Petit.
HELEN'S MOTHER is played by the actor who plays Aunt Chris.

PLACE

San Pedro, California

TIME

The late 1990s
Act One: early September
Act Two: two and a half months later: the week before Thanksgiving

STAGE SETTING NOTE

A wire runs across the length of the set—a professionally rigged wire-walker's wire, with cavaletti ropes and posts. The wire is seen (primarily) by Walter, though other characters may walk it during the play.

FORMATTING NOTE

An asterisk (*) in a character's line indicates the following character's interruption.

AUTHOR'S NOTE

THANK YOU:

I am very grateful to the NEA/TCG Fellowship, under whose auspices this play was written. Thank you: Michael Barakiva, Daniel Alexander Jones, New Dramatists, Lue Douthit, OSF. Richard Howard, I didn't know you when I began this play...but as it turns out, I wrote Walter for you.

This play is for my parents, Mike and Diane Carpenter.

1.

Walter and Helen.

*(**HELEN**'s face is the only thing we see in a spotlight.*

WALTER *is behind her in the dark, adjusting straps and tightening screws.*

Helen closes her eyes.
Stretches her arms out to either side.
Takes a deep breath.)

HELEN. *MIKEY! BREAKFAST!*

(Lights come up.
Kitchen.
Morning.

HELEN *sits on a beach chair, which is atop the kitchen table. Her husband, **WALTER**, is harnessing what looks like a box fan onto the back of the chair, which she is strapped onto.*

Helen wears a postal worker's uniform.)

WALTER. Helen, Jesus Christ, you're blowing out my eardrums!

HELEN. I don't want him to be late on the first day.

WALTER. Just...your voice.

HELEN. This is heavy.

WALTER. I'm working with found materials. The real thing would use an ultra-light metal. What they use for mountain bikes. Titanium alloy.

HELEN. Maybe we should get Mikey a bike for his birthday.

WALTER. I'll make him one.

HELEN. A real bike. Like other kids have.

WALTER. Anyone can have what other kids have. I'll make him something special.

HELEN. Walter, really, I can't stay up here. I can't be late for my route.

These straps are tight.

WALTER. Hold on. This is a test drive. Stand up...

(He turns on the fan. It's loud.)

HELEN. Is something supposed to happen?

WALTER. If we were outside, you'd take a few running steps, jump, and you'd go right up in the air!

HELEN. From a box fan?

WALTER. No, this is a prototype! The real one would be motorized!

I showed you the plans...a parachute.

HELEN. If I'm late Bob gives Shelly my route. Then I'll be stuck with the east side, and everyone there subscribes to way too many magazines. My back is getting cold.

(He takes the fan off her back.)

HELEN. *Mikey!*

(WALTER reacts.)

MIKEY. *(off)* Coming!

HELEN. *Mikey!*

MIKEY. Coming!

(HELEN puts on her mail courier hat, places the newspaper in front of WALTER.)

HELEN. Here's the classifieds.

WALTER. *(absent; working)* Adjust the frame so it doesn't hit the small of the back. *(makes note)*

(HELEN circles items in the classifieds.)

WALTER. Balance the straps higher on the shoulders...

HELEN. Walter, my real husband never ignores me in the morning.

My real husband grinds fresh espresso beans, steams milk, and makes me a latte. My real husband wears a suit and tie even on casual Friday.

My real family makes breakfast before I wake up. They water the lawn, put flowers on the table...

WALTER. Helen, I picked you and you picked me. I'm the one you got. For better or for worse.

(**HELEN** *circles a few more items in the classifieds.* **WALTER** *sketches.*)

HELEN. Did the speech people call?

WALTER. Not yet.

HELEN. They said they would call you by the fifth. That just stuck in my head, because I remembered that was Mikey's first day of school. *(Beat)* Today.

(**WALTER** *sketches.*)

HELEN. You know how I'm going back to school. In real estate. When we have the pension.

WALTER. I've heard the plan.

HELEN. You could go too.

(beat)

WALTER. For what. Real estate? *Land?*

HELEN. For whatever you wanted!

WALTER. I am not– And it's insulting of you to *circle* things! For Christ's sake.

HELEN. There's a real estate course at SPCC that starts next month.

WALTER. Go ahead, enroll.

HELEN. It's an intensive. Nine to four, four days a week. I'd have to lose most of my hours. And we can't…

("Afford that" hangs in the air.)

HELEN. Never mind.

Make sure Mikey eats his breakfast.

(no response)

And call me when you hear from the speech people. Walter?

My real husband always answers right–

WALTER. GOODBYE. "Darling."

HELEN. "Goodbye, darling."

(They share a look.)

HELEN. *(calling out the door a last time)* Mikey! Don't be late!
(She exits. **MIKEY** *enters, goes for the cereal.)*

MIKEY. Hey Dad.

WALTER. Mikey. You ready for the big day? Sophomore year. Not the low man on the totem pole anymore.

MIKEY. School sucks.

Dad, did you like school when you were my age?

WALTER. *(reading)* Mm?

MIKEY. When you were fifteen. Did you like school.

WALTER. I doubt it. But I was thinking about other things.

MIKEY. The war.

WALTER. Yeah.

MIKEY. Did you get a medal in Vietnam?

WALTER. Nope. I was a grunt. Listened to other people tell me what to do for the whole tour.

MIKEY. I should work. Make some bank.

WALTER. Listen, you've got the rest of your life to get some "job." Don't tie yourself down. Be free!

MIKEY. Yeah, free to go to school. Which sucks.

WALTER. Holy cow. Now this is interesting. Would you look at that!

(He shows **MIKEY** *the front page.)*

MIKEY. Some guy on a tightrope.

WALTER. That's Philippe Petit. Greatest wire walker alive. He is walking up a wire that goes from the ground up to the Eiffel Tower. Inclined! He is 2,000 feet above the ground! Can you imagine what he feels like! Jesus.

MIKEY. Does he have a net?

WALTER. He never uses a net.

MIKEY. That seems kind of stupid.

WALTER. He walked between the *Twin Towers* in New York City back in the 70s. I saved the clippings. He's never done anything but walk the wire.

MIKEY. I bet he thought that school sucked too.

WALTER. He's doing exactly what he wants to be doing. You can tell from the picture. Take a look at that wire – he does the rigging *himself.* He doesn't have a bunch of strangers just string it up – he measures the wire, he tightens it – you see those? – those are cavaletti. They anchor the wire. *(in an exaggerated French accent)* "Mon dieu!"

MIKEY. *(laughs)*

WALTER. Mikey. I know high school hasn't been fun for you...

MIKEY. It sucks.

WALTER. I know, but there isn't an alternative.

MIKEY. I could drop out.

WALTER. You're not going to drop out. It'll get better. It will.

MIKEY. I want to be good at something. I'm not good at anything. I want to be good at something, like you were.

(micro beat)

WALTER. When you get home after school, you can help me work on this prototype. *(increased enthusiasm)* A motorized paraglider. A paramotor. *(referring to sketches)* You've got your parachute here – you've got a power* fan to catch the thermal wind–

***MIKEY.** Dad. Dad.

WALTER. You want to try it on real quick?

MIKEY. Dad – there's already a motorized glider. I saw it on TV. These guys are flying across America, they're setting a record for a ton of money. They're called ultralites.

WALTER. "Ultralites," huh.

MIKEY. The gliders are *bikes*, you ride with a parachute on your *back* and then you turn it on and you shoot up into the air. It's crazy.

Probably you have to get a patent or something.

WALTER. Well I was going to once the thing was – I just didn't, it didn't occur to me to do it this early in the process.

– well goddamn.

MIKEY. It doesn't mean anything.

WALTER. Means they got there first.

MIKEY. You were there first, too.

WALTER. I was. *(half to himself)* This is just like the skatekite.

MIKEY. The skatekite was cool.

WALTER. *(staring at the box fan)* Well. The paramotor. May she rest in peace. Onward and upward. Right buddy?

MIKEY. Onward and upward.

    *(**MIKEY** exits. **WALTER** looks at the newspaper.)*

WALTER. *(quietly, to the photo)* "Mon dieu."

2.

Outside steps of San Pedro High School.
Mikey and Maria.
The same morning.

(A **STUDENT** *walks by and shoves* **MIKEY.***)*

STUDENT. Faggot.

*(***MIKEY*** ignores the shove and the student.* **STUDENT** *exits.* **MARIA** *has been sitting nearby, watching. She's visibly pregnant.)*

MARIA. Hey.

(Mikey doesn't answer.)

MARIA. Hey. Hey. Hello.

MIKEY. Oh. Hi.

MARIA. Did you not hear me before?

MIKEY. Didn't think you were talking to me.

MARIA. Well I am. *Comment ca va?*

(No answer.)

MARIA. "How are you."

MIKEY. Oh. Fine.

MARIA. You smoke?

MIKEY. No.

MARIA. Merde.

I don't either. I used to though. I was kind of hoping you were a smoker so I could secondhand it a little bit. I love the smell of other people smoking. People are all like, "Oh my god, the *baby*," and I'm like, "Fuck off." I breathe the *air* in Los Angeles, there's smoke in the air and who knows what else.

MIKEY. I don't smoke.

MARIA. What's your name.

MIKEY. Mikey. Mikey Griffin.

MARIA. How old are you?

MIKEY. Fifteen.

MARIA. That's too old to be called Mikey. I'm going to call you Michael. So. Are you a junior here at glorious San Pedro High?

MIKEY. Sophomore.

MARIA. Me too. I just moved here. How is it.

MIKEY. It sucks.

MARIA. Looks it. Like a goddamn prison.
What do you do around here?

MIKEY. I don't know.

MARIA. What's your story, Michael?

MIKEY. I don't know.

MARIA. Everybody has a personal mythology. Their own symbols. You've got some story.

MIKEY. Doubt it.

MARIA. We can debate it later. Do you have a girlfriend?

MIKEY. *(an inadvertent bark of a laugh, then:)* No.

MARIA. Yeah, I coulda guessed that. No offense. You have a kind face. I've seen the girls around here. Snotty, right?

MIKEY. They can be pretty stuck up, yeah.

MARIA. Those kind of girls always want to call some shit-bag football player their "boyfriend." Kinda guy who'll take you out, get tanked on keg beer playing quarters, then try to shove his hand up your shirt. Pathetic. You shouldn't worry about it too much. Not having a girl-friend I mean. Anybody who peaks in high school is a dismal failure, bound to be on a downward spiral for the rest of their lives. That's what my aunt says, anyway. She says that high school is the worst fucking mess anyone ever has to endure, and that every job that follows is socially simpler, so I'm just waiting it out, you know? I live with my Aunt Chris. My mom tried to kick me out when she found out I was gonna have the sprout. The pitter-patter of little feet would have put a cramp into her booze time. Aunt Chris called my mom a drunk bitch with no sense of responsibility and she said I could move in with her. So I did. Week after I got there, we moved to Sacramento. Me and my mom used to live in Venice in a shithole but it was cool to be near the beach. My aunt's work takes her all over, that's why we went to Sacramento. I've been all over California: Fresno, Temecula, San Diego, San Dimas, Santa Maria, Riverside…this is a big state.

(beat)

I just change schools when we move. Swing with the changes, that's what my aunt says. That's why this dump doesn't faze me.

You don't talk much, do you?

MIKEY. I guess I'm more of a listener.

MARIA. Well, Michael, I think you're very sweet.

I'm Maria.

(They nod at one another.)

MARIA. You know what I like most about you so far, Michael?

MIKEY. No.

MARIA. You haven't said a word about this. *(indicating pregnancy)* Very polite. You wouldn't believe how rude some people are when you're pregnant. They're like, "unwed teen mother…illiterate." Cest la vie. Someday you'll have a girlfriend and she's going to be very lucky, Michael, because she'll see how *tres gentil* you are.

(Little silence.)

MIKEY. Are you an actress. I mean have you ever done any acting.

MARIA. I used to act like I wasn't fucking scared of my mother's belt. *(laughs)*

MIKEY. You don't talk like other people.

MARIA. I'm not like other people. I'm two people. Isn't that amazing? I tell you, being pregnant is the most educational experience I have ever had. Science, psychology, sociology, biology, all rolled up into one event. It's rad. Are you doing anything for dinner tonight?

MIKEY. I'm, I, uh, have dinner with my mom and my dad.

MARIA. Oh. My aunt works a late shift some nights when she's not working from home. I thought you and I might share a meal.

MIKEY. Oh. Uh, I can't. Cause I eat dinner with my family. My mom likes it, you know.

MARIA. Sure. Maybe another time.

MIKEY. *(with heroic effort)* Do you…want to come over for dinner?

MARIA. Okay.

MIKEY. You don't have to if you don't want to, I don't even know what my mom's making.

MARIA. I want to.

I want to.

MIKEY. Okay. Yeah.

MARIA. What's your address?

MIKEY. Um, um, right where I live, um, 1685 Mariposa. Do you know how to get there?

MARIA. I have an excellent sense of direction.

I better go to the office and check whether they have my transfer records. Everyone keeps telling me to take Spanish, they're like, "You're in California." I'm like, I love French. People want an explanation. I want to take French for no reason. I just love the way it feels in your mouth. It's good to love something for no reason. That's the best kind of love. Anyway. 1685 Mariposa.

MIKEY. Yeah.

(She exits.)

MIKEY. Oh. My. God.

3.

Kitchen.
Afternoon, same day.
Walter alone.

WALTER. *(on phone)* Hello? Bill? Hello, Bill.
It's Walter Griffin.

(beat)

The lawn chair guy, right.

How's everything at SoCal Aviation?

Good, good, glad to hear it.

Listen, I was calling to see if you had booked a speaker for the club dinner this year. Because I–

Oh. Well sure. I know I spoke before, but it was a while back, you know, and as I recall Bill you responded pretty positively. I figured you had some new members and it would be worth tossing my hat in the ring.

Well of course – I understand. You don't have speakers back twice, sure. No problemo. Listen, Bill, I wonder if you'd recommend me to other chapters, because, well I can't help feeling that I have a unique story, and it deserves mention. And – did you know that the Smithsonian wants the chair? Yes. Yes. Yes indeed. Well I certainly appreciate it. I'll call those other chapters next week then, after you get back to–

Good to talk to you too.

(He returns to his plans laid out on the table, draws, erases, screws some things together. He talks to himself when he's alone, but easily, naturally, as though he's talking to a friend; he doesn't mumble.)

WALTER. People who have pilot licenses do not fully appreciate being up in the air.

(He works.)

They take it for granted.

(He works.)

How can you take something like that for granted?
To rise up from this earth. To be lifted up.

(**WALTER** *looks up at the wire.*

PETIT *appears on the wire and walks, simply, elegantly.*

There might also be a slide or series of slides shown here – photographs of Petit on the wire between the Twin Towers.)

PETIT. *Bonjour!*

WALTER. Hello!

PETIT. *Everything changes on the wire.*
A bird doesn't use a leash.

WALTER. A bird doesn't use a leash.
When I was a little kid, I went to the fair, and I saw a lady holding a huge bunch of balloons. I thought, man, those would take you up.
I thought about how *I* was gonna fly…all through the army, boot camp.
I just liked to dream about it.

PETIT. *When I walked the wire between the Twin Towers, people understood that they would tell their children about my walk.*

WALTER. I remember.

PETIT. *Taxi drivers left their taxis. Streets were gridlocked. Everyone on Wall Street stopped trying to make money.*

WALTER. They looked up.

PETIT. *A man in the sky, forcing you to dream!*

WALTER. I wish I had been there. And now – your Eiffel Tower walk. You're in every paper.

PETIT. *As you were, mon ami.*

WALTER. It was a long time ago.

PETIT. *People forget. They'll forget me too. You, you are still dreaming.*

WALTER. I am, I am. I keep – searching for the next thing, you know.
I find your work so inspiring, Monsieur Petit.

PETIT. *Philippe. Your inspiration is my reward.*

WALTER. It's hard to turn inspiration into something lucrative, you know?

PETIT. *A bird does not carry a wallet.*

WALTER. A bird does not carry a wallet.

(**HELEN** *enters, puts down her bag.*

PETIT *disappears.*)

WALTER. Amazing. Amazing man. Fearless.

HELEN. Who's that, hon.

WALTER. Philippe Petit.

HELEN. Oh, right, I saw that in the paper. You know, Cynthia asked me if I was *pregnant* today. Okay fine, I had my shirt untucked, but still – pregnant? Then she said "Oh sorry, I guess you're just glowing."

WALTER. Do we have any D batteries?

HELEN. People always say, "You're glowing" to pregnant people because it's not polite to say, "You're fat!"

WALTER. You don't look pregnant.

HELEN. Just fat. *(über-cheerful)* How's the paramotor.

WALTER. Actually I'm going in another direction, I'm using this prototype to lead me somewhere else.

HELEN. Where?

WALTER. Somewhere new.

(**HELEN** *waits.*)

WALTER. I'm not thinking about exactly where. I'm thinking about the best way to make the *next* thing.

HELEN. I think maybe… that's a problem.

WALTER. Please, Helen, don't start.

HELEN. *(quiet)* They're going to cut my hours down. I said please don't and they said not this month but next. They're going to cut them by a third.

Do you want to say anything?

WALTER. What do you want me to say?

HELEN. I want you to say that you're going to find a way to–

I want you to say that you'll get a job.

WALTER. Goddammit. I have a job. I have work.

I mean – Don't you think I'm trying? Goddamn. God-
damn. What do you imagine I do all day?

HELEN. I don't know.

WALTER. I'm working all day, every day. I'm looking for
opportunities.

HELEN. There's a difference between "work" and "opportunities."

WALTER. What's that supposed to mean.

HELEN. I know the counselor said to avoid "you" statements
and focus on positive neutral sentences but – God! I
don't have a neutral sentence in me! You *sketch* all day!
You weld pieces of *metal* together! You – you don't get
any kind of *job* –

WALTER. I gave a presentation at the opening of the City of
Industry Mall two weeks ago –

HELEN. A job, Walter, a place that you *go to* every day–

WALTER. I've *done* that, I–

HELEN. Not in a long time.

WALTER. Just going somewhere, just "showing up" is not –
It's not who I am! It's not what I'm supposed to do!

HELEN. What are you supposed to do? Tell me! What are
you *supposed* to do? When I was a little girl, I did not go
to sleep at night and dream about sorting mail! I'm not
getting any younger. I don't want to get younger, that's
not what I mean. All I want is a moment of breath, just
a, a week of living without feeling like everything in
our life is going to shatter into pieces and float away
– I can't stand that I'm the only one who thinks about
this all the time – *(trying to breathe)*

(She can't breathe. Asthma.)

WALTER. Where's your inhaler. Is it in your bag? Okay, hold
on, stay calm, I'm going to find it…hold on…got it.
Here. Here you go. Just…

*(She inhales and breathes. He tries to rub her back. She
shrugs him off.*

He stands apart from her.)

WALTER. I've been looking for – for opportunities – but they've been – scarce. Somehow I haven't been able to find something, an idea, that matched up with the ideas I have in my–

(searching…)

I want you to *trust* me.

I'm going to find something tomorrow – this week. The *end* of the week, *latest.*

I'm going to find a job, somewhere to go. Okay? I will. I'm going to get your pills. Are they under the sink? Or in the cabinet. Never mind. I'll find them.

(He exits.

HELEN *looks at his plans, closes her eyes.*

MIKEY *enters.)*

MIKEY. Mom?

HELEN. Hi, honey. Just a little flare-up. Allergies. How was your first day of class?

MIKEY. The same.

HELEN. Bet it was good to come back as a sophomore.

MIKEY. It was the *same.*

HELEN. Give it time.

MIKEY. That's what you said last year.

HELEN. I know.

*(**MIKEY** starts to exit.)*

MIKEY. Mom, is it okay if I have a friend over for dinner?

HELEN. A friend. Of course. Of *course* it's okay. When?

MIKEY. Tonight.

HELEN. Tonight? That's *wonderful,* sweetheart.

MIKEY. Mom. Don't freak.

HELEN. What's your friend's name?

MIKEY. Her name's Maria.

HELEN. Oh. *Oh.*

MIKEY. Mom don't. I just met her at school today. Seriously don't freak.

HELEN. You just met her and you invited her over for dinner?

MIKEY. She's new.

HELEN. Oh Mikey. That is so sweet. God I need to get started. What time is she coming over?

MIKEY. I don't know. Dinner time.

HELEN. I need to get some things together. Go get your father, I need him to run to the store...

MIKEY. Mom, I swear if you freak we are not doing this.

HELEN. I am not freaking Mikey!

(She uses her inhaler.)

MIKEY. Oh God.

HELEN. Her name's Maria? Maria what?

MIKEY. I don't know. I just met her.

(starting to exit; turning) You're going to like her, Mom. She's really cool.

4.

Kitchen.
Dinnertime, same night.
Walter, Helen, Mikey, Maria.

(**MIKEY** *stares at his plate.*

WALTER *and* **HELEN** *stare at Maria's stomach.*

MARIA *eats.*)

MARIA. This was delicious Mrs. Griffin. My Aunt Chris doesn't cook very much. Like ever. Sometimes she warms stuff up. This was really nice.

HELEN. Thank you, Maria.

You live with your aunt?

MARIA. Yeah.

HELEN. Your father's sister or your mother's?

MARIA. Oh, my mom's. Nobody knows anybody on my dad's side. Nobody knows my dad, really. So, it's my mom's sister.

HELEN. Have you lived with her a long time?

MARIA. Just since my mom kicked me out. For being pregnant.

WALTER. Oh, you're pregnant?

HELEN. Walter!

I'm sorry. –About your mother.

MARIA. Don't be. My mom's on a pretty unstoppable bourbon binge. Totally destructive. It's way better with my Aunt Chris.

HELEN. Well that's good.

(*They eat.*)

MARIA. So what was Michael like when he was little?

MIKEY. What kind of question is that?

MARIA. I don't know Michael very well yet. Maybe you'll tell me his story.

HELEN. Well...

What was Mikey like. He went down stairs on his bottom until he was three.

MIKEY. Oh. My. God.

HELEN. He'd…*scootch.*

WALTER. *(mischievously)* He was afraid to walk!

MIKEY. This is not happening.

WALTER. Not *afraid:* cautious.

HELEN. Exactly. Cautious. Mikey wanted to do everything right. He waited until he was *sure* he could do it, and then he did, no fanfare or fuss.

WALTER. He didn't learn words one at a time: cat, bat, dad. He was quiet for months and months – he never spoke at all…

HELEN. I worried that he was autistic. But he liked hugging.

WALTER. One day, I think he was about two, two and a half, he turned to me and he said, "I think I'd like a tomato sandwich." Just like that.

MIKEY. This is a ridiculous conversation.

MARIA. It's sweet.

HELEN. And he loved *Peter and the Wolf.* That's all he would listen to. Day and night. Over and over and over. *(**HELEN** sings, sings again.)**

MIKEY. Oh yeah. Until you lost the record. That was such a bummer.

*(**WALTER** laughs and then stops abruptly.)*

MIKEY. No way – you didn't lose it?!

HELEN. You can't imagine how sick I was of that record. It was in my head all the time… *(Helen sings an extended phrase somewhat maniacally)**

MIKEY. I can't believe you! That is so wrong!

HELEN. I tried to sing you other songs, but you wouldn't let me finish.

MIKEY. What songs.

HELEN. Oh you know, *(she sings)*
  Are you sleeping, Are you sleeping
  Brother John? Brother John? Morning bells are ringing –

*Please see Music Use Note on page 3.

MIKEY. Okay!

WALTER. *(to Maria)* Pretty soon you'll have a little one of your own to think about.

MARIA. Yup.

HELEN. How old are you, Maria?

MARIA. Sixteen.

HELEN. And are you going to keep the baby?

MIKEY. *(instantly)* Mom, I really don't think that's any of your business. Man!

HELEN. You're right, I'm sorry of course you're right...

MARIA. No, it's okay. I don't mind. Yes I'm definitely keeping him. Her. I can't wait. But at the same time I wish I could stay pregnant forever. I love it. I never felt this good in my life. It's like, I'm never alone. Crazy. Like I'm the one that's gonna be born. Everything new. Being pregnant's the best thing that's ever happened to me.

(They eat.)

MARIA. What do you do, Mrs. Griffin?

HELEN. I've been a mail carrier for twelve years.

MARIA. Wow. Do you...like it?

HELEN. Some days I think, forget it. I am not walking up one more driveway. And then I say to myself, only eight more years till we can collect my pension. And I walk up the driveway. After you pass the ten-year mark... you don't want to look back.

MARIA. Do you ever read people's mail?

HELEN. No!

Sometimes I peek at a postcard. If it's from somewhere exotic.

MARIA. That would be too tempting. I'd open everything. I'd want to get inside everybody else's lives.

HELEN. I used to have the most wonderful mail route. The houses...the gardens...It was heaven to walk up and down those blocks. Up to each big door. I put the mail in each slot so carefully. Isn't that ridiculous. I'd walk down every long driveway feeling proud, like I did an extra-good job. I didn't care that I was getting home late every night. So it took me longer, so what? But people complained about getting their mail too late in the day. So I was switched.

MARIA. What do you do, Mr. Griffin?

WALTER. I lecture at aviation clubs around the area. I'm an entrepreneur.

(beat)

MARIA. I don't really get what that means.

MIKEY. He's an inventor. Dad, tell her! My dad made a, a kind of flying machine out of a lawn chair before I was born. He was on David Letterman!

MARIA. No way.

MIKEY. Dad, bring her down to the basement and show her the chair!

WALTER. Oh hell, Mikey, no one wants to get into all that.

MARIA. I'd like to see it, Mr. Griffin.

WALTER. Okay, right this way…

HELEN. Mikey, you stay, I need some help with the dishes.

(WALTER and MARIA exit.)

HELEN. Mikey are you that baby's father?

MIKEY. *What?!*

Mom, you're out of your mind. No.

HELEN. You might have mentioned that your friend you were inviting for dinner was pregnant!

MIKEY. I didn't know that was an issue for you and *dinner guests.*

HELEN. Don't you act like I'm crazy! I have the right to know if you are going to be a *father!*

MIKEY. Jesus, Mom, you *are* crazy – I told you that I just met her *today.*

HELEN. Do you "like" her?

MIKEY. Do I – forget it. This is totally weird.

HELEN. I just want you to be aware of the ramifications of getting involved with a girl who is about to become a mother –

MIKEY. *Fuck*, Mom*, we're not "involved!" We don't even know each other! Just because I invited someone to dinner doesn't automatically mean that I want to have *sex* with them!!

*HELEN. Do not use that language, Mikey! –

(*During Mikey's line,* **MARIA** *has entered the room.* **MIKEY** *turns around to see her.*)

MARIA. That chair is pretty amazing.

(**MIKEY** *exits fast without a word.*

WALTER *puffs upstairs, carrying the lawn chair.*
This is the lawn chair which he rigged to make his flight, sixteen years ago. The chair is shabby and dusty, the woven plastic fraying. There are several empty gallon milk bottles strapped to each leg.)

HELEN. Now why did you bring that up here.

WALTER. Maria wanted to hear the story. I thought we'd all stare at it while I told her. Get the full effect.

HELEN. Well sit down, honey. You don't want to be on your feet so much. How far along are you?

MARIA. Six months. How long ago did you ride in this?

WALTER. Sixteen years.
I had been thinking about making a flight on my own since I was a kid. On my very first date with Helen, I said, "There's this dream I have."

HELEN. I thought he was crazy.

WALTER. She thought I was handsome. I had never talked to anybody about it before. Helen had a sweet face. She looked like she'd understand.

HELEN. I was pretending.

WALTER. I said, "I want to do this thing."

HELEN. When I came home that night, my mother asked, how was your date? I didn't tell her about his thing about flying. Or that he had forgotten his wallet. Most people would be embarrassed, it would have ruined the evening. Not Walter.
I said: "I like him."

WALTER. I knew it.

HELEN. He got very animated whenever he talked about the flying. He lit right up. He was – *impassioned*, like, like Galileo.

WALTER. I had dreamed about it forever. I mean literally dreamed. On my tour of duty in 'Nam, I'd be slogging along in the mud, miserable, and then I'd just go inside my head: boom: up in the sky.

MARIA. Um. Did you think of, you know, getting a pilot's license?

WALTER. Oh no no no. This was something I had to do my own way. I had already been in the army. Rules everywhere. I wanted to get up there on my own and...just be free.

(**MIKEY** *enters and sits quietly, listening.*)

WALTER. So, time goes by, I convinced Helen to marry me. The night before the ceremony – do you remember this?

HELEN. Of course I remember.

WALTER. The night before the wedding, Helen asks me if I still think about – you know, going up. I said you bet. She looks at me. I guess she was thinking 'for better or for worse.'

A year later, almost exactly a year, I fell asleep after a long day. And I saw *myself* in the sky, sitting in a chair tied to a bunch of balloons. Balloons! A giant bunch of balloons! I sat straight up and said, "I know how to do this."

MARIA. That's crazy.

HELEN. That's what I said.

WALTER. Clear as day, in my dream. Next day, boom, I went to Sears, bought the lawn chair. Eleven dollars. I went to the hardware store, bought forty-two balloons. four-fifty each. Weather balloons. Each of them was seven feet across, had a pull of twelve pounds. I engineered a system. Strapped 'em all to the chair.

MARIA. How were you gonna come down?

MIKEY. He had a BB gun.

WALTER. An air pistol.

MIKEY. He was going to *shoot* each balloon out.

MARIA. *(re: the gallon jugs on the chair)* What were these for.

WALTER. Ballast. Filled 'em with water so the chair wouldn't be tossed around in the wind. Gets windy up there.

MARIA. Oh my gosh.

WALTER. I started filling up the balloons the night before. Took three tanks of helium. The backyard looked wonderful. Balloons everywhere.

HELEN. My mother thought he had post-Vietnam stress syndrome.

WALTER. She loved it.

HELEN. Hardly. I was pregnant with Mikey. I was terrified. I was thinking, why is he doing this? Does he want to leave his wife and baby?

WALTER. That is so dramatic.

HELEN. Well that's what I was thinking!

WALTER. Once I got up in the air, my heart was pounding. It was exactly like my dream. I kept floating up. At two thousand feet, it got real quiet. Soon I couldn't hear anything but the sound of the sky. I don't know how to describe it. I could see everything: mountains and desert, the whole Pacific Ocean, sparkling blue.

MARIA. Did you take a picture?

WALTER. I had a camera, but I didn't use it. This was just for me.

(MIKEY runs out.)

HELEN. Where is he going? Mikey!

MIKEY. *(off)* I'll be right back.

WALTER. I kept going up. I thought I was drifting towards Mojave, maybe. I could see the Angeles National Forest. Incredible. Trees spread out way below me like a carpet. I checked the altimeter. 2,500 feet. Next time I checked, 6,000, 7,000. I kept going higher.

MARIA. Were you scared?

WALTER. I was – awed. Too happy to be scared. Too much to see.

MARIA. How high up did you go?

WALTER. I got up to 16,000 feet. That's about three miles. I could see a little plane, way below me. Tiny! The air was thin. You can't imagine! My feet were numb. I thought, okay, time to come down a bit. Shot out seven balloons, pop, pop, pop. I put the air pistol in my lap to check the altimeter. And then a gust of wind pushed the chair, and the thing fell out of my lap.

MARIA. Did it hit anyone?!

WALTER. Not that I know of.

HELEN. Thank god. I hate this part.

WALTER. I watched it getting smaller and smaller. Gone. I thought, "Huh." In a total emergency, I had a parachute, I could jump.

HELEN. You had used that parachute exactly *once.*

(**MIKEY** *enters holding a tape recorder.*)

MIKEY. I got the tape!

(*He turns it on.*)

MIKEY. At 13,000 feet, his CB radio went off, and this air controller radioed him. This is the tape!

WALTER. Son of a gun. I was wondering where that was.

HELEN. I can't believe you still have that thing.

(*They listen.*)

RECORDED CONVERSATION

(*STATIC/RADIO AIR*)

OPERATOR. Please repeat.
What airport did you take off from?

WALTER. I, uh, I didn't take off from an airport, buddy.

OPERATOR. Who am I speaking with? Who is the pilot?

WALTER. This is Walter Griffin.

OPERATOR. I need to have the name of the *airport*, Sir. *Departure* and *destination.*

WALTER. Uh, okay, my point of departure was 1633 West Seventh Street, San Pedro.

OPERATOR. Say again the *name of the airport.* Please repeat.

WALTER. The thing is, guy, uh, I'm sorry, but this is an unauthorized balloon launch. I'm not in a plane.

OPERATOR. A *balloon* launch?

WALTER. Yes.

OPERATOR. ...What color?

(*pause*)

WALTER. They're red.

(*pause*)

OPERATOR. There is more than one balloon?

WALTER. I guess I have about 35 of them left, yeah.

OPERATOR. Did you say you are piloting a *cluster* of 35 balloons?

WALTER. Right. I am piloting a cluster. My name is Walter Griffin. I made a launch out of my backyard this morning at 10:30 a.m.

(*pause*)

OPERATOR. Sir, hold on please.

(*to someone else*) Bobby, go get Alan, he's not gonna believe this.

(**MIKEY** *turns the tape off.*)

WALTER. So. I'm up in the chair thinking...do I use the parachute? Then – the helium started to leak from the balloons. – I drifted down, down, down. I started hearing all the sounds of the normal world again. Cars, trucks honking. Kids playing. Then I started to lose altitude, but fast. I slashed the water gallons. The ground was coming up. I was thinking, oh, man, here we go. I came down fast, scraped across this guy's roof, and the balloons got tangled up in the power lines. I was left hanging in the chair about eight feet above the ground.

MIKEY. So cool.

HELEN. They had to shut down the electricity for *four blocks*. And the police came.

WALTER. Officer looked at my driver's license, sat and stared at me for a while, and said, you know, I can't think of what the citation might be. So you're free to go.

HELEN. Well the FAA didn't feel that way.

WALTER. Ahhh, the FAA... *(waves his hand dismissively)*

HELEN. And you know what? He *gave* that chair away. To some kid in the neighborhood. He didn't even know him!

WALTER. He asked if he could have the chair as a souvenir, I wasn't thinking.

HELEN. I put an ad in the paper and he came over and returned it. Thank god.

WALTER. The Smithsonian wants it in their museum collection.

MARIA. Are you in the *Guinness Book of World Records*?!

(A little moment.)

WALTER. It was, the launch was "unofficial... " so it couldn't be a record...

(They all look at the chair.)

HELEN. My real husband always takes care of dessert.

WALTER. "Who wants ice cream?"

HELEN. Why don't you and Mikey go to the gelato place on Third.

*(She gives **WALTER** money.)*

HELEN. Maria and I will make tea.

WALTER. *(to **MARIA**)* Sit in the chair if you want.

*(**MIKEY** and **WALTER** exit. **HELEN** clears plates.)*

HELEN. Go ahead, dear. Sit in the chair.

*(**MARIA** does. There's something magic about sitting in the chair.)*

HELEN. Do you have a doctor here?

MARIA. Yeah. My aunt found me a really good doctor.

HELEN. And after the baby's born...she's going to help you?

MARIA. Definitely. My aunt really has her act together, total opposite of my drunk mom. She, my aunt's like you.

HELEN. She is?

MARIA. Like, you have your act together. Anyway I'm excited. Making a family.

HELEN. Walter always wanted to have a family. For better or for worse. I guess it made me feel serious about him, because a man talking about a family was so – strange. My mother could tell something was up. One night when I came home, as soon as I walked in the door, she was waiting. She asked me point blank:

(HELEN'S MOTHER *appears. She speaks to Helen;* HELEN *speaks to* MARIA.)

HELEN'S MOTHER. Are you going to marry him?

HELEN. I said, "I don't know, I hope so."
My mother didn't say anything. And I said, "What. What? If you're going to tell me not to marry him, I don't want to hear it."
She said,

HELEN'S MOTHER. Helen, do what you please, but you need to listen.

HELEN. I said "Well what is it then."
She said,

HELEN'S MOTHER. Make sure he loves you more.

HELEN. I said, "More than what?"
She said,

HELEN'S MOTHER. More than you love him.

HELEN. I said, "That's *ridiculous*, we're going to love each other the same."
She said,

HELEN'S MOTHER. It never works out that way. One person

needs to love the other person more. One person needs to hang on a little harder. It's not sweet, but that's how it is. Marry a man who loves you more.

(**HELEN'S MOTHER** *disappears.*)

MARIA. How come you're telling me this.

HELEN. I was angry at my mother when she said all that to me. I said, "that's none of your business." But. It's not such bad advice.

MARIA. I'm never getting married. Who needs it. No offense.

Seems like you got what you wanted.

(*A little moment.*)

MARIA. It is so cool to think about. A baby. New eyes. New ideas. I mean the sprout's not even *here* and already I'm thinking whoa, I need to learn to *cook*. So I can do that family thing, right? Breakfast. Lunch. Dinner. You've got that wired. I'm going to switch chairs, this isn't totally comfortable.

5.

Basement. Afternoon.
Walter.

(**WALTER** *sits at a table, going through bills. Perhaps he uses a calculator. He writes a check and seals it in an envelope, making note of the payment in the registry. He takes a dollar bill out of his pocket, contemplates it, and meditatively tears it in half.*

PETIT *appears, walking the wire.*)

PETIT. *I lay down on the wire to look at the clouds. The world was far below me. Everyone on Wall Street stopped trying to make money.*

(**WALTER** *tears the dollar halves into small pieces. He throws the pieces of dollar into the air like confetti.*

PETIT *juggles.*)

PETIT. *A man in the sky!*

(*With sudden violence,* **WALTER** *kicks the paramotor or some other project and it breaks – a window? – anyway it makes a giant crash. After a moment, he begins to clean up quietly, as if someone else made the mess.*)

HELEN. *(off)* Walter? Are you okay?

WALTER. Fine. Everything's fine. Don't come down.

6.

SPLIT SCENE.
Maria's house / Mikey's house.
Maria, Mikey, and Aunt Chris / Walter and Helen.
That same evening.

*(IN MARIA'S HOUSE, Loud rocking country music –
preferably old [real] country music: Johnny Cash, Hank
Williams Sr., George Jones, Ernest Tubb...Wayne the
Train Hancock would be fine, too.**

AUNT CHRIS *and* **MARIA** *perform a lengthy and elabo-
rate country line dance.* **MIKEY** *watches. Despite her
pregnancy,* **MARIA** *dances with agility.*

After the music stops, they both sit heavily. **MARIA**
clutches her tummy. **AUNT CHRIS** *fires up a cigarette.
Her demeanor is bone-dry.*

She holds out a cigarette to **MIKEY**, *who shakes his head
"no.")*

MARIA. He doesn't smoke.

AUNT CHRIS. Pieced that together, sweetheart.

MIKEY. That was um, impressive.

AUNT CHRIS. Picked up line dancing in Reno, Nevada. God
DAMN that's a shithole but you gotta do something to
get outta your room. I taught some routines to Maria
because what the fuck's the point of doing a line dance
alone?

MARIA. Aunt Chris, do the one you got named after you.

AUNT CHRIS. Maria, I'm going to finish my cigarette. Then
we'll see. So you're in Maria's class.

MIKEY. We have geometry together.

AUNT CHRIS. A subject you're basically assured never to
encounter again in your lives.

MARIA. You have to know what ninety degrees means.

AUNT CHRIS. It means hot.

MARIA. The *angle*. Ninety degrees is a right angle.

*Please see Music Use Note on page 3.

AUNT CHRIS.	MARIA.
Maria, nobody likes a smartass…	Yeah right,
Except me.	Except you.

AUNT CHRIS. Sweetheart, why don't you go into the kitchen and look for some pate and shit for our guest.

MIKEY. Uh, just the pate, thanks.

AUNT CHRIS. He's funny.

MARIA. Tss. We don't have anything like that.

AUNT CHRIS. See what kind of facsimile you can come up with, baby.

(MARIA exits. AUNT CHRIS stares at MIKEY, smokes.)

AUNT CHRIS. What's your story, kiddo? You rich?

MIKEY. No.

AUNT CHRIS. Poor?

MIKEY. I don't know. Kind of.

AUNT CHRIS. What's your dad do?

MIKEY. He invents things.

AUNT CHRIS. Well he's the reason you're poor.

MIKEY. The stuff he invents is really cool.

AUNT CHRIS. Could I go into a store and *buy* something he made?

MIKEY. Patents are really complicated.

AUNT CHRIS. Kiddo, you're poor because your dad isn't making it, and your mom's job, whatever it happens to be, is carrying you.

MIKEY. So. So what.

AUNT CHRIS. Why don't I give you a reading.

(From a hidden place, she reveals a deck of tarot cards.)

AUNT CHRIS. Never had a reading? Tarot cards?

MIKEY. How come you want to.

AUNT CHRIS. Passes the time.

(MARIA enters.)

MARIA. I told you, we don't have anything in the…ohmygod

are you going to read Michael's cards? Oh, Michael, you'll love it. She reads my cards every week, and she reads the baby, too. You're not afraid, right?

MIKEY. Ch. No.

AUNT CHRIS. We could teach you to line dance.

MIKEY. Let's read.

(**AUNT CHRIS** *lights a candle from her cigarette. Taps the deck three times.*)

AUNT CHRIS. Sit there, kid, we need to look at the cards from the same angle.

Hold the deck in your left hand, choose a card with your right.

Lay it down.

(*He does it.*)

AUNT CHRIS. The Wheel.

(*She and* **MARIA** *look at each other significantly.*)

AUNT CHRIS. Describe what you see.

MIKEY. Looks like a game show prop. Wheel of Fortune. It's upside down.

AUNT CHRIS. Reversed. We call that reversed.

Tap it three times.

One, two, three.

Something's been triggered.

Because the card is *reversed*; that means your *dreams* have started it.

What's been on your mind lately, dear?

(**HELEN** *enters. She moves around the kitchen, taking out sandwich makings, salad items.*)

HELEN. (*calling*) Walter? Mikey!

(*no answer*)

MIKEY. I don't know.

AUNT CHRIS. Nothing you can do to stop it now. The wheel's been spun.

MIKEY. I'm supposed to find a wheel of fortune to spin?

AUNT CHRIS. You *are* the wheel. Close your eyes for a minute, focus your thoughts.

(**HELEN** *finds a note.*)

HELEN. "Mom. I'm at Maria's. Back by ten."

AUNT CHRIS. *(rapidly laying out the cards)*
This covers you.
This crosses you.
This is before you.
This is beneath you.
This is behind you.
This crowns you.
These are your dreams.
This is the outcome...

(**MARIA** *and* **CHRIS** *look carefully at the cards.* **AUNT CHRIS** *whistles.*

HELEN *gives up on the sandwiches, pours cereal into a bowl, eats it dry.*)

MARIA. Wow. Wow.

MIKEY. What. What?

MARIA. You have ALL major arcana cards except for the pentacles!

AUNT CHRIS. Luck. Abundance. Fortune. Change. Bounty. In short, money. Lots of money.

MIKEY. I don't get it.

AUNT CHRIS. Lemme break it down for you. This card is you. Wheel of Fortune. What covers you. The Lovers.

MARIA. Is he going to meet a girlfriend?

AUNT CHRIS. Maria. Let me do this reading. The Lovers card doesn't necessarily mean people. Two or more forces are aligning, moving towards a common goal. Ring a bell?

MIKEY. Okay.

AUNT CHRIS. Okay. Lovers cover, Money crosses, Judgment is beneath, Hermit is behind. Let's talk about the money. King of Pentacles. Kings are all about *releasing*. Like they say "let it go." Pentacles equals *financial patterns.*

MIKEY. I don't have a, a "financial pattern." I don't have *finances.*

AUNT CHRIS. *(moving cards)* Pentacles, finances – more more more – back to the Wheel of Fortune, and we got the Star, beautiful, good resources, and the High Priestess reversed, don't worry it's not religious, it means you got the intuition fired up. Judgment beneath, Hermit behind, The Star crowning, High Priestess before. And your dreams are The Tower – ooh boy. And here's the outcome.

MIKEY. What "outcome."

(WALTER enters.)

HELEN. Walter!

WALTER. Don't start.

MARIA. *(a bit awed)* The world.

HELEN. You're dressed up.

WALTER. I found a job.

HELEN. You did? You found…oh Walter…did you go back to the–

WALTER. Someplace new. It's not a big deal.

HELEN. It is a big deal, it's wonderful.

AUNT CHRIS. The World. Everything's available to you, kiddo. You reach out, the Golden Ring's in your fist. It's raining luck. That's your reading.

(AUNT CHRIS smokes thoughtfully.)

WALTER. Let me just – I've been driving a long time. I need to eat something.

HELEN. I started to make sandwishes. Sandwiches.

WALTER. I'll do it.

(WALTER begins to make a sandwich.)

MARIA. You are *so* psyched.

AUNT CHRIS. You want a job?

MIKEY. Are you messing with me?

AUNT CHRIS. Kid. Seriously. Why don't you come work for me.

MIKEY. You'd hire me because of a reading.

AUNT CHRIS. I've hired people for worse reasons.

MIKEY. I'm not good at anything.

AUNT CHRIS. You will be. Wheel of Fortune.

MIKEY. I have to go to school.

AUNT CHRIS. After school. Before school. Weekends. You're lucky. Cards say so. I pay attention to luck.

MIKEY. What do you do?

AUNT CHRIS. I'll teach you.

HELEN. What will you do?

WALTER. I'll work.

MARIA. I have to study.

AUNT CHRIS. So study, Sweetheart. Mikey, sit tight.

> (**MARIA** *and* **AUNT CHRIS** *exit.* **MIKEY** *stares at the tarot cards.*)

HELEN. I mean – the job. What are you doing? Where is it?

WALTER. North. It's a long drive. I need to change.

> (**WALTER** *exits.*
>
> **AUNT CHRIS** *enters, hands* **MIKEY** *a phone.* **MARIA** *studies her French textbook.* **AUNT CHRIS** *drops a fat phone directory in Mikey's lap.*)

MARIA. *Fumer* "to smoke"
Tomber "to fall"
Monter "to go up"
Descendre "to go down"

AUNT CHRIS. Source material.

MIKEY. A phone book?

AUNT CHRIS. You call businesses. Ignore garages, plumbers, and repair shops. You want white collar. Car dealerships are okay.

Read your script. Stick to it until you get a feel.

MIKEY. *(reading from script)* "Hi. This is blank calling from The Office Supply place… "

AUNT CHRIS. Don't say "blank" say your name, stupid.

MIKEY. "Hi. This is Mikey – This is Michael – calling from The Office Supply Place? Who am I speaking with today? …Anna? Hi, *Anna*, how are you doing? *Anna*, are you the person in your office who makes the decisions about ordering supplies? You are? Great? Well listen *Anna*, I'm calling today? Because I want you to know that we've got a gift for you?"
Is this legal?

AUNT CHRIS. It's office supplies, not crystal meth. "The Office Supply Place," that's the name of my business.

MIKEY. Everyone in the phone book's your customer?

AUNT CHRIS. Sooner or later. "The Office Supply Place, Incorporated" – get it? When you call them for the first time, you say, "Hi, I'm calling from The Office Supply Place." They think it's their regular supplier and then they reorder with me. Simple. Legal.

MIKEY. Why do I say I have a gift?

AUNT CHRIS. People are more compelled to buy shit if they get something for free. Psychology.

MARIA. *Je ne fume pas.* I don't smoke.

MIKEY. What do I say if they ask me what the gift is?

AUNT CHRIS. They never ask.

MARIA. *Personne ne fume.* No one* smokes.

***AUNT CHRIS.** No one ever asks.

> (**WALTER** *enters, different clothes, resumes eating.*)

MARIA. *Rien ne change.* Nothing changes.
Rien. Nothing. *Personne.* No one.*
Qui est á la maison? Personne.

HELEN. Tell me everything.

WALTER. It's an office. Like any office anywhere. Chamber of Commerce.

HELEN. Chamber of Commerce where, in Long Beach?

WALTER. Los Padres.

MARIA. *Je n'ai pas d'argent.* I don't have any money.

MIKEY. How do I make money?

HELEN. Los Padres.

AUNT CHRIS. You work on commission. You get a percentage of everything you sell.

WALTER. Do we have any ham?

MARIA. *Je n'ai jamais d'argent.* I never have any money.

MIKEY. A percentage. That's it?

AUNT CHRIS. Kiddo, three weeks in Fresno I moved a hundred and fifty thousand dollars of merchandise.

MIKEY. What's my percentage?

AUNT CHRIS. Five percent, hit this number, I bump you up to seven.

*(She writes on a pad, shows **MIKEY**.)*

AUNT CHRIS. Your could make over a thousand a day.

MIKEY. How do people spend *that much* on office supplies?

AUNT CHRIS. People need pens.

MARIA. *Je n'ai ni argent, ni cigarettes.* I have neither money nor cigarettes.

MIKEY. I'll, okay, I'll do it. Deal.

AUNT CHRIS. A deal from the Wheel. Start tomorrow, come over at five a.m.

MIKEY. What's open at five a.m.!

AUNT CHRIS. New York, Rhode Island, and Pennsylvania. I'm nationwide.

MARIA. *Aimez-vous voler comme un oiseau?*
Oui, j'aime voler.

HELEN. Is that up near Santa Barbara? How did you find it?

MARIA. *Do you like to fly like a bird?*
Yes, I like to fly.

WALTER. I put on a suit and got in the car. Didn't know where I was going to go. Just got on the freeway. I got on the one-ten at Gaffey Street. Drove north. I merged onto the four-oh-five, after thirty-six miles, it turned into I-five. I thought, there are opportunities out here. I drove for an hour, maybe – and then. Los Padres, population five thousand thirty four. Chamber of Commerce.

HELEN. "The Los Padres Chamber of Commerce." That sounds so – official. Oh Walter it's *great*.

AUNT CHRIS. Memorize your script, get it natural.

WALTER. It's on the edge of the Los Padres National Forest. Right past Gorman. Beautiful area up there. I talked with HR, told them a little bit about me – what I've done. And they were pretty taken, you know? They said – let's take a flier. Let's do it. So I'm going to be a liaison for any new businesses in the area.

MIKEY. What happens if I'm on the phone and…

WALTER. Were there any messages today?

AUNT CHRIS. And they say no.

HELEN. No.

AUNT CHRIS. Then you lose the commission. You want to be a closer, keep them on the phone.

MIKEY. Keep them on the phone.

MARIA. *Je connais mon pere.* I know my father. – Ha! No I don't.

Je ne connais pas mon pere.

HELEN. It's just amazing, The "business liaison." When do you start? How many people work there? I can't believe that you just drove and found it – how much are they going to–

WALTER. Don't *talk* it to death!

MARIA. *Regrettez-vous quelque chose?*

Are you sorry?

WALTER. …sorry.

MARIA. *Non, Je regrette hein.*

HELEN. It's all right.

MARIA. *Oui, je regrette tout.*

(AUNT CHRIS *lights a cigarette, watches* MIKEY, *smokes.* MIKEY *mouths the words of the script, silently, practicing.)*

WALTER. It's temporary. I'm getting other opportunities going.

HELEN. I know.

WALTER. I'll need the car.

HELEN. I'll carpool with Cynthia.* That's not a problem.

*__MARIA.__ *Nous savons notre problem.* We know our problem.
Je n'ai pas d'argent.

HELEN. I'm so proud of you.

WALTER. *(quietly)* Thank you.

> (**MIKEY** *practices his phone spiel very, very softly. When he comes to the end, he repeats.)*

MIKEY. *(near-silent)* *"This is Michael calling from The Office Supply Place. Who am I speaking with today? …Karen? Well hi, Karen, how are you doing?"*

> (**MARIA** *stops suddenly, closes the book, holds her tummy. Mikey's pitch stops.)*

MARIA. She kicked! Hello there! Hi.
Bonjour, mon enfant! It's me, *ta mere.*

WALTER. Something about this gives me a sense of – possibility.

HELEN. Good.

MIKEY. *(near-silent)* Karen may I ask you, are you the person in your office who makes the decisions about ordering supplies? You are? Great! Well listen Karen, I'm calling today with a special gift for you! Would you confirm your address for me? Great. Karen, I've got this gift…

MARIA. *(singing softly, overlapping)* Frère Jacque
Frère Jacques
Dormez-vous? Dormez-vous?
Sonnez le matin Sonnez le matin
Din, dan, don
Din, dan, don

> (*During Maria's song,* **PHILIPPE PETIT** *appears on the*

wire.)

MIKEY. *I'm sending it out to you at that address, and, uh, I hope you enjoy it! One more thing while I've got you on the phone. Can I refill any of your standing orders for, say, liquid paper and post-its? How about tape dispensers? Have I told you about our special on pilot felt-tips, a gross for ninety-eight dollars..."*

(**HELEN** *joins Maria's song. They sing beautifully: in a round, of course.* **MIKEY** *continues on the phone.)*

MARIA. *Frère Jacques*
    Frère Jacques   **HELEN.**
    Dormez-vous?   *Are you sleeping*
    Dormez-vous?   *Are you sleeping*
    Sonnez le matin   *Brother John?*
    Sonnez le matin   *Brother John?*
    Din, dan, don   *Morning bells are ringing*
    Din, dan, don   *Morning bells are ringing*
    Din, dan, don   *Ding, dang, dong*
    Din, dan, don   *Ding, dang, dong*

(**WALTER** *sees* **PETIT** *on the wire. He gazes up at Petit's walking, rapt.)*

End of Act I

ACT 2

7.

Three months later.
November, the week before Thanksgiving.
Aunt Chris & Maria's house.
6:00 a.m.

*(**MIKEY** speaks on a headset, pacing, taking notes on a clipboard, absurdly confident.)*

MIKEY. *(laughing)* …you're not going to regret this Frances, this is a one-of-a-kind deal I'm giving you on tape dispensers. So. I get the twelve cases out to you today – the shipping's on me. Would you confirm that order number for me sweetheart…twenty-three C thirty-five-oh-one, excellent…and Frances you look for that gift in about a week, and make sure to call and tell me how much you like it, okay? Great.

*(He hangs up. **AUNT CHRIS** enters with a cup of coffee and cigarette. She's dressed in a fabulous kimono or other glamorous sleep attire.)*

MIKEY. The state of Delaware is being very good to me. It's cool that I came over this early, right? I wanted to kill some sales before school.

(She looks at his clipboard/notes.)

AUNT CHRIS. *(whistles)* It's *fine* that you came over, kid. Keep 'em moving up.

MIKEY. Is Maria here?

AUNT CHRIS. It's six in the A-fucking-M. Yeah she's here. *Sleeping.*

MIKEY. Right, sure. Ha ha.

What are you guys doing for Thanksgiving?

AUNT CHRIS. We'll be eating hospital turkey if Maria decides to pop.

MIKEY. You want to come over? For, for Thanksgiving dinner?

AUNT CHRIS. That's sweet.

I'll check with Maria, okay? Decide in the moment. You want another cup?

MIKEY. Yeah, okay. Do you think I could get paid sometime soon?

(AUNT CHRIS sizes MIKEY up.)

AUNT CHRIS. I thought you wanted me to hold it for you.

MIKEY. I did. But…I think um I want to have it now. If that's okay.

AUNT CHRIS. Let me guess. You want to buy a car.

MIKEY. You're going to think it's stupid.

AUNT CHRIS. Try me.

MIKEY. Um. I want to show my dad.

It was a good idea for me to keep the job, uh, low-key for a while. But now. I think I, I want him to see.

(beat)

AUNT CHRIS. Well why don't I cut you a check right now.

MIKEY. It was so cool of you to hold it. They wouldn't have got it. Before. But when I show my dad that check, my name on it? It's going to be awesome. Show me my total again.

AUNT CHRIS. You *know* your total.

MIKEY. Please.

(AUNT CHRIS sighs, but she's enjoying this. She takes out an adding machine.)

AUNT CHRIS. Here's September.

(She punches numbers into the adding machine, shows him.)

AUNT CHRIS. October.

(She punches numbers into the adding machine, shows him.)

AUNT CHRIS. November, up to yesterday.

(Punches numbers into the adding machine.)

AUNT CHRIS. So...your total...

(She shows him the result.)

MIKEY. That is so cool.

AUNT CHRIS. I'll get my checkbook.

(As she exits...)

MIKEY. *(calling)* Um, I guess I'll just roll calls for a little while longer, and when Maria wakes up we can leave for school together.

AUNT CHRIS. *(calling)* Free country.

*(**AUNT CHRIS** exits. **MIKEY** dials.)*

MIKEY. Good morning, who am I speaking with? Hi, Jan, this is Michael at the Office Supply Place, how are you today?

*(**MARIA** enters. She's very very very pregnant.)*

MARIA. Morning.

MIKEY. Oh hi. Hi.

(on phone) Jan I just want to confirm your business address.

*(to **MARIA**)* Did I wake you up?

MARIA. *(shaking her head no)* I have a French test today. Last night I fell asleep before I finished studying.

MIKEY. *(on phone)* Great! Jan, that all sounds good I'll-get-back-to-you-about-that-wishing-you-all-the-best-bye. *(hangs up)* Do you, do you want some help? With studying.

MARIA. Is that how you close all your sales?

MIKEY. I sold a lot this morning already. Anyway, do you want help?

MARIA. You take *Spanish*.

MIKEY. I could quiz you.

MARIA. It's not vocabulary, it's reading comprehension.

MIKEY. Oh.

MARIA. I guess I could tell you about this little French story, that might help. Let me get my book.

(She starts to exit, turns.)

MARIA. You're like the hardest worker my aunt has ever had.

MIKEY. Really?

MARIA. In Sacramento she had like 6 people working out of the basement and I don't think that all of them put together made what you're making.

MIKEY. How's your...

MARIA. The baby? No kicking yet this morning. *Pas de problem.*

MIKEY. Are you getting nervous?

MARIA. No. This is what I'm made for. I'm built to be a baby *machine.* Think about it, there's ancient shit going on here.

MIKEY. I guess, right.

(As **MARIA** *exits...)*

MARIA. God. I can't believe you get here so early, you're obsessed.

(She exits, passing **AUNT CHRIS**, *who might touch her cheek.)*

AUNT CHRIS. *(re: the check she's holding)* This going to get you into trouble?

MIKEY. No. No way.

AUNT CHRIS. Okay. Here you go. Fifty-nine thousand four hundred dollars and change.

MIKEY. Man.

AUNT CHRIS. I'll confirm this week's orders by Wednesday, go to the bank, and make the deposit. You give good phone, kiddo.

MIKEY. *(staring at the check)* Thanks.

AUNT CHRIS. *(pointedly)* Look at that, you've still got an hour before school.

(She exits. He dials, looking at his check.)

8.

Walter's bedroom.
Same morning.

(**PETIT** *walks the wire. He strolls, he sits, he walks and looks at the birds in the sky.*

WALTER *irons a tie. He glances up at Petit, watches him on the wire.*)

PETIT'S VOICE.

Here is why I don't use a net.

One. It has never crossed my mind.

Two. The man who falls off a wire gets what he deserves.

Three. There is freedom in solitude.

Do you know how you are going to die?

I will be walking on a wire, just like always, an ordinary day, and I will begin to walk up the inclined wire, up, up, walking effortlessly. And I will walk into the clouds. And then I will be gone.

(**WALTER** *begins to iron a $20 bill. He holds it up, lights it on fire. He watches the bill burn, then drops it, stepping on the ashes. After a moment, he drops to his knees to clean it up.*

HELEN *enters, also getting dressed.*

Soon after Helen enters, **PETIT** *is gone.*)

HELEN. It starts this week. Cards. "Family newsletters." Catalogs catalogs catalogs. From now through January, people are gift wrapping *phone books* or *bricks*.

WALTER. They're mailing presents.

HELEN. Bags of dry cement. Blocks of Italian marble. Rocks. No one ever stops to think, "Someone has to walk *five blocks* with this stupid oversized package."
What are you doing?

WALTER. Dropped some change.

HELEN. You look nice today. (*checks her watch*) The traffic's going to be hell for you.

(**WALTER** *shrugs.*)

HELEN. I hate that you have to drive so far.

WALTER. It's simple: get on the one-ten from Gaffey Street, go north. Merge onto the four-oh-five. Becomes I-five after thirty-six miles, Drive for an hour, freeway gets quiet, and just past Gorman – there it is. Los Padres. On the edge of the Los Padres National Forest.

There's a holiday party next month. For the families. You and Mikey can come. Eggnog. Carols.

HELEN. Have you noticed that Mikey's been getting up early every morning? Really early.

WALTER. Mm-mm.

HELEN. He's gone before I get up. He comes home late, he gets up early…

WALTER. Helen, leave him alone. He wants to be left alone.

HELEN. Do you think that he's having sex with Maria?

WALTER. She's pregnant.

HELEN. You can have sex when you're pregnant.

WALTER. They're just friends.

HELEN. Would you talk to him about it please.

WALTER. No!

HELEN. You're his father! I don't think it's great that he's spending so much time with her.

WALTER. First he doesn't have enough friends to suit you, now he has a friend. You would find a way to worry if he took up with Jesus Christ.

HELEN. Well who would want to see their friend crucified.

My real husband comes up with an answer to this problem.

WALTER. Well let's call him and hear the solution.

HELEN. He's already at work making lots of money.

WALTER. Mikey is fine.

(*A horn honks outside*)

HELEN. (*re: the honking*) Cynthia.

WALTER. Wait. I almost forgot.

(He takes out a bracelet, puts it on her wrist.)

WALTER. You like silver.

HELEN. Walter. It's beautiful. You are ridiculous and it's beautiful.

Have a good day at work.

WALTER. Say hi to that handsome husband of yours.

HELEN. "Hi." Bye.

*(***HELEN*** exits.*

A twenty-dollar bill falls down from above. **WALTER** *turns and watches it flutter to the ground.)*

9.

Mikey's house.
The next day. Afternoon.

*(***WALTER*** has the lawn chair up on the table. He's scrubbing off the rust, cleaning it up.* ***MIKEY*** *enters.)*

WALTER. There he is!

MIKEY. Dad. You're home.

WALTER. I decided to take the afternoon and do something I've been putting off too long.

(He gestures re: the chair)

Sprucing it up before I call up the Smithsonian and hand it off.

*(***MIKEY*** *watches* ***WALTER*** *work.)*

MIKEY. *(gesturing)* What's that?

WALTER. Oh, that's oxalic acid. Rust remover. Give it a scrub, rust comes right off.

MIKEY. See, perfect example of why school is lame. They don't teach anything useful. Oxalic acid. I'm learning geometry. A subject I'm basically assured never to encounter again.

WALTER. You want to give me a hand? I could use help. If, if you're not on your way out.

MIKEY. No. I mean, yeah. Yeah.

WALTER. Grab a rag.

(They work on the chair.)

MIKEY. Today in English we had to write "hope statements." Like, what we "hope" to achieve in higher education and what we "hope" to accomplish later in life. It was dumb.

WALTER. Oh. I want you to do whatever you want to do.

MIKEY. What if I wanted – just to work?

WALTER. I don't want you to feel tied down.

MIKEY. I wouldn't feel tied down if I liked my job.

WALTER. No, sure.

MIKEY. What was your first job?

WALTER. *(considers)* I was ten, and we had a neighbor, Mr. Hendrickson. He used to give me fifty cents for picking up after his dog. And in high school I delivered pizza. Drove around in this crummy old van and delivered pizzas and hoped that people would tip.

MIKEY. Were you good at it?

WALTER. *(shrugs)* Delivering pizza? I dunno. Guys in my class, the big thing was, you know, buy a shiny car and then spend all your time and money making it shinier. I didn't care about that – about being a slave to the dollar.

MIKEY. And, when you were my age, did you think about, like, what work you were good at?

WALTER. Mikey, I'm going to tell you a secret. It's the secret of life. The secret of life is, almost every job is *exactly the same* as every other job. Picking up someone else's shit. I've tried a lot of jobs. Everything reminds me of when I was ten years old. Walking around Mr. Hendrickson's yard with a shovel and a bucket. Be your own boss. That's what I think.

(They work on the chair.)

MIKEY. When you're your own boss, the one thing I don't get is, um, who pays you?

WALTER. You pay yourself. You make your own way. You understand what I'm saying?

MIKEY. Kind of.

Did you ever try to sell the chair?

WALTER. *(laughing)* No.

MIKEY. Seriously, if a museum wants it I bet you a, a collector would want it, too. You could totally sell it, make an insane profit.

WALTER. I doubt that.

MIKEY. I bet you could! You should totally advertise.

WALTER. It's not for sale.

MIKEY. I know it's not. I was just saying.

WALTER. *(re: Mikey working on the chair) Careful.*
Just...watch what you're doing.

*(Knocking. **WALTER** answers the door — it's a **UPS MAN**.)*

UPS MAN. Walter Griffin? Sign right here.

*(**WALTER** signs; the **UPS MAN** tosses two large bundles in the room and leaves.)*

MIKEY. What are these?

WALTER. Open it up.

*(**MIKEY** pulls a length of red silk out of one bundle.)*

MIKEY. Omigod omigod they're PARASAILS! No way!

WALTER. How do you like that, huh?

MIKEY. We're going to *fly* these?!

WALTER. In three days, on Thanksgiving, we'll drive out to the desert, unpack 'em, and take em' up!

MIKEY. Oh my god. Are they *motorized*?

WALTER. These operate entirely through the power of wind. They're *pure*.

MIKEY. Man these things *new* are like a thousand dollars each!

WALTER. What do you care how much they cost?

(beat)

MIKEY. I don't "care," I –

WALTER. What's that supposed to mean, "a thousand dollars!" They're top of the line!

MIKEY. I didn't fucking mean anything.

WALTER. Don't you talk that way to me, Mikey!

MIKEY. My name's Michael, Michael, Michael!

*(**MIKEY** runs out.*

***WALTER** picks up the parasail and stares at it.)*

10.

Mikey, Maria.
The next day. Afternoon.
Maria's house.

(**MARIA** *rummages around, munching on snacks.*)

MARIA. There's this children's book we're reading in French, it is so fucking marvelous. It's about this girl named Claire, and through the whole book she's standing with her back to you, and the whole page is *black.* She's a tiny thing in the corner of these two giant black pages. It's like, there's just this *kid* standing in the *dark.* Sometimes a moon appears, or a train, but basically it's a kid alone in the dark. "Claire amit la nuit." That means, Claire loves nighttime. This book would never be published in America. We only want kids to see a sunny day and that's pretty much it.

MIKEY. In Spanish all we ever read about is Pedro and, like, trips he goes on.

MARIA. *"Mais dans le gare de Clare les trains ne bouget plus."*

(**MARIA** *stops abruptly.*)

MARIA. God I need to sit down for a minute.

MIKEY. You're not gonna have it now, are you?

MARIA. She's just moving.

MIKEY. So…are you guys coming over for Thanksgiving?

MARIA. Your family is like, a mirage.

MIKEY. My parents are screwed up.

MARIA. You think so.

MIKEY. Yeah.

MARIA. They're not punching you, or trying to have sex with you, right.

MIKEY. Jeez, Maria. That's gross.

MARIA. Are they?

MIKEY. *No*-wuh.

MARIA. I don't want to, you know, minimize the difficulty of your family life, but frankly: it could be worse. Coming from the unwed teen mother perspective.

MIKEY. Right.

MARIA. Can I ask you a question.

MIKEY. Sure.

MARIA. Are you a virgin.

MIKEY. Tss. NO.

MARIA. You can tell me.

MIKEY. I *would* tell you. I'm not.

MARIA. You're not.

MIKEY. No.

MARIA. You've had sex with someone.

MIKEY. Yes.

MARIA. Who?

MIKEY. Don't *laugh* at me.

MARIA. I'm not laughing, Michael. I just want to know: who?

MIKEY. You don't know her.

MARIA. So fine, tell me who.

MIKEY. This girl.

MARIA. Are you in the CIA? Is she in the witness protection plan? "This girl." What the fuck, Michael. Tell me. Who'd you have sex with? Just say it.

MIKEY. Why don't you say who *you* had sex with.

(Pause.)

MARIA. Okay.

MIKEY. I'm sorry.

MARIA. I'll tell you.

MIKEY. I shouldn't have said that.

MARIA. I just said I'll tell you.

MIKEY. You don't have to.

MARIA. I *know* I don't have to! I'm *pregnant*, Michael, I'm not *porcelain*. I'm not going to break because you asked who the baby's father is.

My mom thought it was *her* gross boyfriend. That's what she was *afraid* of.

That's why she kicked me out.

*(**MIKEY** looks at her.)*

MARIA. It wasn't him.

MIKEY. That's good.

MARIA. There was this person at school. My old school. This guy. "Jared."

He was a senior. He played tennis. He was going to go to some Ivy League college on scholarship. Pretty much a Ken doll who could walk and talk and drive. And play tennis.

Anyway, I was a freshman. And like, everyone was looking at me all the time. Because of the girls. It was crazy. One day, I'm some low-rent nobody who wears clothes from T.J. Maxx, the next day, I'm like Ms. *Popularity*. With the guys.

I knew I was going to lose it eventually, right. The question was, how? Like my mom? She had her story, she told it endlessly, how she got nailed in the back of a *truck* and the guy spit on her afterwards. It was her anthem. "Give it away, see what it gets you." And I was thinking, not me. I can *choose* how it happens. I can write my own story. It's going to happen, so I'm going to figure out the best way. So I chose. I looked around at all the girls who wouldn't give me the time of day, and I thought, who do *you* want? And they all wanted Jared. That's who I picked. Weird that it was so easy.

So, "Jared and Me." We did it. A lot. We'd go different places. Sometimes hotels. Sometimes his house. He was nice. That was unexpected. He talked to me like an actual human being. Treated me like a precious object, at least when we were alone. I thought, oh, I chose *right*. It was – fun. Then I missed my period. I wasn't like, the bad cop of contraception and neither was he.

MIKEY. Where is he now?

MARIA. *(shrugging)* College I guess…

MIKEY. Does he know?

MARIA. Yeah, I told him. He completely flipped, and then I said Jared don't *worry* about it, I wouldn't fuck up your shiny golden future, no one will ever know it was you. He was like, *really*? And I said, hey, my body, my

business. And he went, oh, Maria, you are a wonder.
He called me a wonder.

(**MARIA** *might be crying.*)

MIKEY. Are you...are you okay

MARIA. It's so fucking *stupid.* He wasn't even a truly nice
person, the day after I told him he stopped speaking to me and the week after that he wasn't in school
anymore. He's just some jock I allowed to get into my
pants and that makes me as deluded as every other
pathetic girl at our school. Deluded and pregnant.

MIKEY. Well...you loved him. Right?

MARIA. I don't know. No. Yes. I don't know. There's no
reason.

MIKEY. What did it feel like.

MARIA. Oh, god. Well obviously it's different for me than it
is for you. But the first time it hurt, not a lot, but kind
of like an intense pressure –

MIKEY. NO. No, not – I meant, being in love.

MARIA. Oh.
I felt floaty. Special. Chosen. Even though I chose him.
That's stupid. It's all so stupid.

MIKEY. Would you ever look for him?

MARIA. Oh yeah sure. I'm going to call a *stranger,* introduce
him to a baby he doesn't want. That's deciding: yeah,
Maria, let's have some pain. Here's a perfectly happy
baby – let's fuck her up a little. Dad wants to be left
alone and so does the baby and so do I. Why would I
do that?

MIKEY. I don't know. Sorry. Sorry.

MARIA. *Don't be sorry!* I *hate* sorry, there is nothing worse
than *sorry.* I *wanted* to tell you. Get it? You didn't *make*
me. You're my friend. I'm not sorry for anything.

MIKEY. You're not?

MARIA. No. I have this baby inside of me, this baby that I
made. She's going to understand me, and I'm going to
understand her like we're twins. Twin stars.

(*Little pause.*)

MIKEY. I'm a virgin.

MARIA. I know.

MIKEY. Nothing has ever happened to me.

MARIA. Something will.

MIKEY. I love you.

(*They stare at one another.*)

MARIA. Oh…Michael.

MIKEY. I love you more than–

More than–

I don't know what.

I think you should – you should let *me* be the father.

I know you don't love me the same way, that's okay I don't care. It doesn't matter. I want to be with you when you have the baby. Don't say anything. Just think about it. I have this check. It's a lot of money. It can be for the baby, the baby's clothes and education and everything. I'll do the birth coaching, I'll go to extra coach classes to catch up. I think I'd be good at it. Being a father. I could be really, really good at it. I'll take French. If you want. Here.

(**MIKEY** *gives her the check. He places it in her hand, closes her fingers over it.*)

MARIA. Wanna feel her?

MIKEY. How come you say "her?"

MARIA. Woman's intuition. Give me your hand.

(**MARIA** *takes Mikey's hand, places it on her tummy. The baby kicks.*)

MIKEY. Oh. Wow.

(*He puts his head on her tummy, listens.*

MARIA *takes his hand and places it on her breast.*

MIKEY *sits up.*)

MIKEY. Um.

(**MARIA** *places her hand over his. He tries to pull away, but she holds his hand there.*)

MARIA. It's okay.

(She kisses him.)

MIKEY. I love you.

MARIA. I know.

(She kisses him again.)

11.

The wire.
Mikey, Petit.

(MUSIC: Beyond the Sea [in the original French].

PETIT *walks the wire, not acknowledging the music. Then:*

MIKEY *skips across the wire. He dances. He does a trick. He kneels on one knee, bowing his head with honor and grace at the completion of the walk.* **PETIT** *bows back.)*

12.

That evening.
Helen, Mikey.
Mikey's kitchen.

(**HELEN** *sits at the kitchen table. She looks shell-shocked,*
very strange. Maybe she keeps picking things up and
putting them down again. Maybe she makes a sound
that's almost like crying but not crying. Her demeanor
is disconcerting. Papers and torn envelopes are scattered
on the table.

MIKEY *enters whistling "Beyond the Sea.")*

MIKEY. Bonjour!

HELEN. Where have you been? Where do you go every
morning and every night?

(**MIKEY**'s *startled by her tone.*)

MIKEY. Mom, chill out.

HELEN. You are my *son* and I never know where you are –
where were you tonight? I want you to tell me. Now.

MIKEY. I, I've been with Maria.

HELEN. You're with her in the morning, you're with her at
night. What are you doing with her at six o'clock in
the morning. I wake up and you're *gone*. Are you on
something? Do you take drugs?

MIKEY. No. No! I have a job.

HELEN. What do you mean you have a job. You manage the
cross country team. What job.

MIKEY. I work for Maria's Aunt, I was going to tell you but I
wanted it to be a surprise.

(**HELEN** *stares.*)

MIKEY. Aunt Chris gave me a job.

HELEN. You have a job...perfect.

(*little bark of a laugh: weird*)

MIKEY. You're acting...I don't know. What's wrong?

HELEN. Where do I start. What's wrong. What's wrong?
Well today I drove to Los Padres. I thought it would
be fun to surprise your father. I borrowed Cynthia's
car. Drove. Two hours. I tried to find the Los Padres

Chamber of Commerce. There's no Los Padres Chamber of Commerce. There's no Los Padres. It doesn't exist.

MIKEY. You probably drove to the wrong place.

HELEN. *There isn't a place.*

I passed Gorman. I bought a map at a gas station. I asked people. I called information. I drove home and I started going through our papers to see if there was an address on a paycheck. I didn't find any paycheck stubs, so I kept looking through everything–

(**WALTER** *enters, wearing a suit and carrying a briefcase. Silence. He looks at them.*)

HELEN. What do you do?

WALTER. Good evening to you too.

HELEN. Answer me. What do you do?

WALTER. What do you mean, what do I do.

HELEN. What do you do, Walter, it's not a confusing question. What. Do. You. Do. You get up you shave you take the car you leave the house every morning, what do you do after that?

WALTER. Mikey, why don't you go to your room.

HELEN. NO you stay right here, you need to hear this.

WALTER. Hear *what.*

HELEN. I want you to explain to your family what you *do* every goddamn day. Because you don't go to "Los Padres." Are you having an affair?

WALTER. Am I – no.

HELEN. What have you been *doing.*

WALTER. What does it matter.

HELEN. Just say it. Say it. You tell me. You don't do anything. Right?

MIKEY. Mom…

HELEN. Be quiet! *(to Walter)* You ANSWER ME.

WALTER. What does it matter?

HELEN. What does it *matter?* YOU INVENTED A TOWN. "I get on the one-ten from Gaffey Street. I merge onto the four-oh-five, it becomes I-five after thirty-six miles. Just past Gorman." Every day for the past *three months* that you've left the house has been a lie, it–

WALTER. A lie that you enjoyed! A lie that – I mean, tell me Helen, did you ever really care what I did? Or where I went? As long as I brought in money, you didn't ask a thing!

HELEN. "Brought in" money! Brought it in. Do you think I'm an idiot?

WALTER. No, I–

HELEN. You're wrong! You're wrong I AM an idiot, I AM, because I *wondered* where the money was coming from but I didn't *check!* You said "direct deposit" and I bought it. And that makes me a goddamn idiot.

MIKEY. I don't get it.

WALTER. *(to* **MIKEY***)* It's gonna be all right.

HELEN. Tell me how!

You've been taking money out of our *savings*. Out of the *pension*. For months, you've been withdrawing everything I've saved, and it's gone now.

All of it.

I mean you've been taking out money and giving it to me as if it was money you *earned*. Like a crazy person. Why did you do that?

WALTER. I'm going to make it up.

HELEN. We will be taxed for every single occasion you made a withdrawal, there are huge *penalties* – it's not only that the money's gone, it's that we have to PAY for you taking it! I saved twelve years, tell me *how* you're going to make it up, tell me, are you going to build a *submarine* now? Sixteen years after the precious lawn chair, he finds Atlantis!

MIKEY. Mom.

HELEN. I wish it *was* an affair, I wish it *was, who* makes up a job – forget it, a *town*, who allows a *thing*, a *chair* to define his life, instead of people! I don't have any idea of what to do in order to – TELL ME I'M BEGGING YOU, WHAT DEFINES YOUR LIFE!

WALTER.

What do you know about what defines my life!

MIKEY.

STOP IT STOP BEING SUCH A JERK!

MIKEY. WHY DO YOU HAVE TO BE SO LAME, MOM?! DAD WANTS TO DO BIG THINGS!

(**HELEN** *stares.*)

HELEN. Congratulations. You spent the last three months lying to me, devastating our savings, and I'm the jerk. Kudos.

(**HELEN** *slams out the door.*)

MIKEY. Dad?

WALTER. Yeah.

MIKEY. Is it true.

WALTER. *(abruptly)* Yeah.

MIKEY. What'd you do with the money.

WALTER. I just withdrew it, gave it to your mother. Like it was a weekly paycheck. She seemed to want that. I bought those parasails. Thought they'd be fun. I, ah. Got the car fixed. Strange how it all goes.

MIKEY. We can take the parasails back.

WALTER. Sure, sure.

MIKEY. Dad. I have to go out.

(*No answer.*)

MIKEY. I'm going to make everything okay.

WALTER. Everything *is* okay.

(**WALTER** *takes out a dollar bill, tears it in half meditatively, not really paying attention to Mikey.*

MIKEY *runs out.*

WALTER *tears a small corner of the bill. He places it in his mouth, chews.*

He picks up his briefcase, opens it, and places the torn-up pieces of the dollar in the case. There are many shredded dollars there.

WALTER *closes the briefcase, looks inside the cardboard box, and begins sifting through the clippings.*)

13.

Aunt Chris & Maria's place.
That same evening.

MIKEY. Hello? Hello! Maria? – Aunt Chris? Maria! Hello!

(The room is empty and pictures on the wall are gone.
There is a phone cord but no phone.

MIKEY *walks around, bewildered.*

On a single table in the middle of the room is an enve-
lope. **MIKEY** *picks up the envelope. It's addressed to him.*
He opens it and reads.

MARIA *appears. She sits easily on the wire above, holding*
her tummy.)

[NOTE: Maria and Michael don't hear each other in
this scene, although they might see one another.]

MARIA. Dear Michael,
So if you're reading this, we're gone.
I don't know where. Aunt Chris never tells me till we
get there.
I'm bummed you won't be around to coach me when
I have the sprout. You'd be a great coach. I have a feel-
ing. But don't worry about me. I'll be okay.
About the money. Aunt Chris had *no idea* you'd make
so much.

*(***AUNT CHRIS*** appears in a separate light, smoking*
thoughtfully.)

MARIA. She said,

AUNT CHRIS. If he was over eighteen, he'd be coming with
us.

MARIA. Seriously. You were awesome. She's really sorry
about the money...
Her needing to take it I mean.
I feel awful.
It's not fair.
I don't know what to say except I'm sorry. The worst
word. Michael, you're good at something big. Some-
thing most people can't do.

MIKEY. She took my money?

AUNT CHRIS. Money's energy.

MARIA. ...and she needs it, and she's pretty certain that she needs it more than you, so I have to go with that.
She wanted you to have this.

(She drops a tarot card. MIKEY *picks it up off the ground.)*

MIKEY. "The Tower."

MARIA. Remember. Your reading. That was your dream. Aunt Chris said,

AUNT CHRIS. He's in for a change. A big one.

MARIA. Like a supernova.

AUNT CHRIS. Everything old will be swept away.

MARIA. A clean slate. Look at it upright, not reversed.

*(*MIKEY *examines the card closely.)*

MIKEY. This building's coming down. People falling out of it.

MARIA. Don't be literal, Michael.

AUNT CHRIS. The Tower illustrates *impact.*

MARIA. Everything around that tower?

AUNT CHRIS. Nothing's going to be the same.

MARIA. It's *significant.*

MIKEY. How do I find you?

MARIA. Me and Aunt Chris have never been anywhere twice. I'll tell the baby all about you, Michael. Michael, who is *tres gentil,* and courteous, and waiting for something to happen to him. Someday – who knows – you'll be sitting on a bench somewhere, and you'll look up, and there we'll be.
I'm sorry.

MIKEY. You're fucking sorry?

MARIA. I am.

*(*AUNT CHRIS *disappears.)*

MIKEY. I hate you.
I hate you.
I just wanted to nail you.
I hate you!

*(*MARIA *disappears.)*

14.

Later that evening.
Walter's kitchen.

(**WALTER** *sits at the kitchen table. He's still going through a cardboard box filled with files and clippings. They cover the table.*

HELEN *enters. She's been crying.*

WALTER *looks up; returns to his box.*)

HELEN. Is Mikey in his room?

WALTER. He went out.

HELEN. What? Where.

WALTER. I don't know.

HELEN. Jesus. We need to call Maria's house.

WALTER. He'll come back.

HELEN. Why are you so sure? Why would he?!

WALTER. Because this is his home.
This is what we have. This family. This house. This backyard.
A place to come back to.
Are you going to leave?

HELEN. I don't know.

WALTER. How long have you had such – contempt for me?

HELEN. I don't.
I think, I'm afraid you're losing your mind.

WALTER. *(a question)* I'm crazy.

HELEN. I, I don't know. "Los Padres?"

(**WALTER** *doesn't answer.*)

And you're going through a box of crap…That doesn't seem normal.

WALTER. This coming from a woman who has an *imaginary family!*

HELEN. That's different, it's *funny*, it's a *joke*.
How did, how did you go through everything.

WALTER. I just did. I don't really know.

HELEN. Did you *gamble?*

WALTER. I just gave it to you. Like it was a paycheck from a job. That's all.

It wasn't that *much.*

HELEN. It was all we had. You must have known I would find out. What were you planning to say?

WALTER. I wasn't planning anything. I was just buying time. So I could look for opportunities. I didn't think about it.

HELEN. You didn't think about it.

WALTER. *DO YOU WANT TO TALK, OR JUST POINT OUT HOW STUPID I AM!*

HELEN. *I'm trying to understand!*

WALTER. I was trying to do the right thing! Is it so impossible to believe that?

I mean I graduated high school, I was in the army, I created something that got me in the newspaper. How many men can say that! *I did something worthwhile, something that meant something to me.* I didn't think about what it would "get" me. I just made it and it worked. Does that mean I've *used up* my chances? In your eyes, all my options are gone!?

HELEN. No.

WALTER. I don't believe you! Everything about you says resentment!

HELEN. I just want to figure out what has happened–

WALTER. *I'm telling you! I'm telling you!* You're not listening! Why is it that you think your way is the *right* way? Automatically! Because it's *yours.*

HELEN. That's not what I'm saying.

WALTER. You have no respect for me! You could give a good goddamn about what I want to do!

HELEN. WHAT DO YOU WANT TO DO! WHAT!

WALTER. I'M FIGURING IT OUT!

(*A disheveled* MIKEY *enters the room, but from downstairs, not outside.*)

HELEN. Where did you come from?

MIKEY. Downstairs.

HELEN. Your father said you went out.

MIKEY. I'm back.

HELEN. You cannot go running around without telling us where you are.

MIKEY. *You* did.

HELEN. I know it's been a very upsetting night.

MIKEY. I'm fine.

HELEN. Were you with Maria?

MIKEY. I was out.

HELEN. You should have *called home.*

MIKEY. There wasn't any phone. There wasn't anything. They moved.

HELEN. Who moved?

MIKEY. I went to Maria's house. It's empty. Like burglars were there. No furniture. No phone. They're gone. Whatever. Everything is okay. It's just money, right?

HELEN. "It's just money" – what? What does that mean?

MIKEY. I made bunch of money.

I told Maria that she could have my money, and that I'd be the father if she wanted me to. Now she's gone.

HELEN. You'd "be the father?" What are you talking about?

MIKEY. I DON'T KNOW, Mom, why don't we ask *Dad?* What am I talking about?

WALTER. Mikey, what's going on, son?

MIKEY. Define "father." I told Maria that I would do it. Be the father. Help. Change diapers, I don't know. Provide, be some kind of provider. "The Father." Where do I get all that, you know? You don't do very much. You don't do anything.

HELEN. *MICHAEL GRIFFIN. You apologize to your father right now.*

MIKEY. No! What has he ever done but sit at that table and fuck around with things that don't work!

HELEN. He has *loved* you. That's what he does. *You go to your room!*

MIKEY. No! *I had a job!* And the whole time, I felt like I had new eyes or something. Like I could. You know. Provide. I made so much money. Why should I help *you? You're* supposed to be the one helping *me*, I'm just a kid! And I got a job! I thought everything could get better. And nothing did! It's all bullshit. Right? Once you get a job, you're just picking up someone else's shit, so you might as well pretend. Just like we pretend to be a family!

WALTER. That's* not true

***HELEN.** *(overlapping Walter)* Something's burning. Something's burning.

WALTER. Nothing's burning, * the *fire alarm* would go off.

***HELEN.** *(overlapping Walter)* I *smell* something.

MIKEY. I burned it.

HELEN. You burned *what.*

MIKEY. I burnt Dad's stupid chair* in the basement.

(Smoke detector sounds.)

***WALTER AND HELEN.** You did *what? You did what?* What did you just say?

MIKEY. *Go ahead, hit me, you care more about the fucking chair, right?*

WALTER. No, Mikey – oh, Jesus–

(WALTER *runs out and down the stairs.)*

HELEN. Mikey what did you do?

MIKEY. It *melted*. The chair didn't even *burn*. Nothing even *happened*. Nothing ever happens!

(Smoke.)

WALTER. *(from off)* Helen, get the extinguisher! Jesus – call the fire department!

HELEN. Where's the phone. Mikey...

MIKEY. There wasn't any *fire.*

HELEN. *(calling)* Walter?

(Siren alarm from far away.)

15.

The same night.
The curb outside the house, across the street.
Walter, Helen, Mikey, Firefighter.

(**HELEN** *breathes into her inhaler. She is over an asthma attack.* **MIKEY** *wears a blanket over his shoulders.* **WALTER** *sits. They all watch the fire.*

A soot-eyed firefighter stands with them.)

FIREFIGHTER. Do you have anybody you can stay with, Ma'am.

(*No answer from* **HELEN**.)

FIREFIGHTER. We can get you and your family to a shelter for the night if you need it.

HELEN. We can't get back inside?

FIREFIGHTER. We need to put it out, and then we need to secure the scene. We'll send someone in there with you once it's secure.

HELEN. Is the whole house...

FIREFIGHTER. The fire damage is extensive. Then there's the water damage…

Any idea how this happened?

HELEN. It was an accident.

MIKEY. No it wasn't.

HELEN. That's enough.

FIREFIGHTER. Ma'am?

HELEN. I asked my son to dispose of some garbage in the basement, and he misunderstood me. An accident.

FIREFIGHTER. We need to take a report.

HELEN. I just told you what happened.

FIREFIGHTER. We'll need more specific information.

But we can ask those questions in a little while.

(*to* **WALTER**) Sir? Are you all right?

WALTER. Sure.

FIREFIGHTER. Son?

MIKEY. I don't want to talk right now.

FIREFIGHTER. You all stay back here. We'll let you know when it's secure.

(Firefighter exits.)

WALTER. You could move in with your other family.

HELEN. That's not funny.

WALTER. Tell me something incredible that your real husband did today. Did he send you a hundred roses? Did he buy you a new summer home in the South of France? *I'm not kidding, Helen, I need to hear what he's up to!*

HELEN. My, my real husband, he…I'm sorry.

MIKEY. Don't be sorry, sorry's *stupid.*

WALTER. Michael.

MIKEY. Sorry's for suckers.

(WALTER grabs MIKEY with force.)

WALTER. *Everyone's sorry, Michael! You're sorry over and over and over again and you say so.*

MIKEY. Ow!

Fuck you!

(MIKEY begins to cry, puts his face in his arms.

MIKEY tries to shrug him off, but WALTER embraces him anyway. MIKEY cries.)

MIKEY. *(muffled)* Get away.

WALTER. Oh Buddy. I didn't mean to hurt you. I'm sorry. Go ahead and cry.

MIKEY. Dad.

I had this job. I worked every morning and every night. I sold office supplies. And I was good at it. It was the only thing I was ever good at.

HELEN. You're good at lots of things, sweetheart…

MIKEY. No I'm not. I was just good at this *one* thing.

WALTER. *(fierce)* Well then, you're lucky. People search their whole lives to find one thing they're good at. To find the thing that makes them special. You found something. I'm proud of you.

(**FIREFIGHTER** *enters.*)

FIREFIGHTER. Mrs. Griffin. We're ready for you and your son now – we need to get a statement.

MIKEY. I just. I wanted to show you. How I was good at something.

FIREFIGHTER. If you'd go right over there and talk to the fire inspectors.

(*The firefighter gestures towards where Helen and Mikey should go.* **WALTER** *doesn't move.*)

HELEN. *(to* **WALTER***)* Walter. We'll come back.

(**MIKEY** *and* **HELEN** *exit.*

The firefighter takes off his equipment, wipes the soot off his face, and becomes **PHILIPPE PETIT.** **PETIT** *looks at Walter with great compassion. He smiles.*)

PETIT. *Bonjour.*

(**WALTER** *sees that it is Petit.*)

WALTER. Hello. Hello.

PETIT. What's this?

(**PETIT** *gestures to a bundle on the ground.*)

WALTER. A parasail.

PETIT. Je ne comprend pas "parasail."

WALTER. You harness it on your back, and if there's a wind, it lifts you up, you fly.

PETIT. *Quelle incredible!*
Marvellous. You will show me, oui?

(**WALTER** *puts the parasail on.*)

WALTER. *(apologetic)* Some parasails have motors…

PETIT. Birds don't have motors.

WALTER. That's true. I haven't tried flying this before…

PETIT. You have a feel for these things.

WALTER. *(like a child)* Do you think so?

PETIT. Oui.

WALTER. I always felt like I was good at making things. I never took any engineering classes, but I could always look at something and figure out how to make it work.

PETIT. Show me.

WALTER. The idea is, you begin to run, and you leap up, and the parasail billows out behind you...

PETIT. You can do it. You need to do it. You're ready!

WALTER. I'm ready.

PETIT. Don't look down!

On three:

One.

Two.

Three.

(**WALTER** *runs, the parasail strapped on his back.*

The enormous parasail expands, billowing out, covering everything: the house, the street, the sky.)

16.

FIFTEEN YEARS EARLIER.
Walter and Helen's back yard.
Morning.

(The chair – shiny, brand-new – floats, tethered to a tree; it hovers a foot or so off the ground.

We can see the ropes to the balloons above but not the balloons themselves.

YOUNG HELEN *is twenty-two years old, very pregnant.*

HELEN'S MOTHER *stands with her arms folded.*

YOUNG WALTER, *29, checks the lines holding the chair, checks the ballast.)*

YOUNG WALTER. Almost ready!

YOUNG HELEN. Do you have your air pistol, honey?

YOUNG WALTER. Check.

HELEN'S MOTHER. When the police come and arrest you, Walter, *I am not going to stop them.* Helen, tell him that I'm not going to stop them.

YOUNG HELEN. I'm pretty sure he heard you mother.

HELEN'S MOTHER. I don't understand how you can do this to her when she's carrying your *child!*

YOUNG WALTER. I said she could come if she wanted.

HELEN'S MOTHER. Jesus Christ.

YOUNG HELEN. You've double-checked everything, right.

(**WALTER** *is putting on a vest with lots of things tied to it, lots of pockets stuffed full of things.)*

YOUNG WALTER. Maps, compass, altimeter. Triple check.

YOUNG HELEN. And you swear you'll use the parachute if anything goes wrong. Swear it.

YOUNG WALTER. I swear.

YOUNG HELEN. If you don't come down I'll have to move in with my *other* husband, and he's a bore.

YOUNG WALTER. I never want you to live with your other husband.

YOUNG HELEN. Me neither.

YOUNG WALTER. So I'm going.

YOUNG HELEN. So go.

YOUNG WALTER. I love you. *(to tummy)* See you soon, buddy.

YOUNG HELEN. We have the radio so *talk* to us on it.

HELEN'S MOTHER. You're crazy, Walter! You need help. We can get you help!

> *(***WALTER*** blows ***HELEN'S MOTHER*** a kiss.)*

YOUNG WALTER. *(into his CB radio walkie-talkie)* Checking one two. Checking. Checking one two three.

YOUNG HELEN. I mean it. I want to hear from you the whole time.

YOUNG WALTER. I'm getting in.

> *(He gets in the chair.* ***HELEN*** *and her reluctant mother steady it for him as he climbs in.)*

YOUNG WALTER. All set.

YOUNG HELEN. Are you sure?

YOUNG WALTER. Untie the ropes!

> *(***HELEN*** starts to untie the ropes. As she does:)*

YOUNG WALTER. This is the greatest day of my life.

> *(And the chair holding* ***YOUNG WALTER*** *sails up and out of sight.* ***HELEN*** *and her* ***MOTHER*** *watch.*
>
> ***MOTHER*** *shades her eyes. After a minute,* ***HELEN'S MOTHER*** *picks up binoculars and stares up, searching.)*

HELEN'S MOTHER. Jesus, that was fast.
Oh my god he's tiny already. Helen tell him to come down.

> *(***HELEN*** picks up the CB radio.)*

YOUNG HELEN. *(into radio)* Walter, it's Helen. Do you copy?

HELEN'S MOTHER. For god's sake…

YOUNG HELEN. Walter, Do You Copy? I love you, do you copy?

(The radio goes SHHH and then yelps with sound, louder than expected.)

WALTER. *(ON THE RADIO)* Helen, this is Walter. I copy.

YOUNG HELEN. Walter, you're so far up!

(Radio static.)

WALTER. *(ON THE RADIO)* Oh. It's wonderful up here. I can see everything so clearly!

YOUNG HELEN. We're getting a little nervous, Walter. Maybe you should come down now!

WALTER. *(ON THE RADIO)* I dreamed about it up here, but I had no idea it would be this beautiful. If I didn't ever have to come down, I wouldn't! This is…this is something else.

YOUNG HELEN. We're waving at you Walter, do you see us? We're waving.

(Radio static.

HELEN *and her* **MOTHER** *wave.)*

End of play

PROPERTY LIST

Scene 1
Beach chair, kitchen table, box fan with straps, postal worker's uniform & hat; newspaper, cereal, bowl, spoon, plans, pencil, eraser, screwdriver

Scene 3
inhaler

Scene 4
Dinner plates & silverware; lawn chair with plastic gallon milk cartons attached

Scene 5
Bills & envelopes, calculator, check, envelope, registry, dollar bill, project (to kick), window (to break)

Scene 6
Cigarettes, deck of tarot cards, candle, sandwich makings and salad items, cereal, bowl, phone, French textbook, phone directory, script, pad

Scene 7
Clipboard, headset/phone, cup of coffee, cigarette, sleep attire, adding machine, check

Scene 8
Iron, tie, $20 bill (to burn), watch, bracelet, $20 bill (to fall)

Scene 9
The Chair, cleaning stuff/oxalic acid, two bundles, a clipboard to sign, red silk

Scene 10
Snacks, check

Scene. 11
Music

Scene 12
Papers, torn envelopes, briefcase, dollar bill (to tear/eat), many shredded dollar bills, cardboard box/clippings

Scene 13
Phone cord, envelope/letter, cigarette, tarot card

Scene 14
Box and newspaper clippings

Scene 15
Inhaler, blanket, firefighter equipment, parasail bundle (that opens/ expands to cover everything)

Scene 16
The Chair, tethers with ropes leading up to balloons (NOTE: balloons mayor may not be visible), vest with items tied to it and many tools in may pockets; binoculars, walkie-talkies (2)

Also by
Bridget Carpenter...

Fall

The Faculty Room

Please visit our website **samuelfrench.com** for complete
descriptions and licensing information

Breinigsville, PA USA
02 November 2009
226863BV00003B/1/P